AF824758

MONTHLY BUDGET

THIS BOOK BELONGS TO

MONTHLY BUDGET

Monthly Income **Month:____________**

Income (Source 1): $________

Income (Source 2): $________

Total Monthly Income: $________

Charity

Tithe/Giving: $________

Saving

Emergency Fund: $________

Retirement Fund: $________

Housing

Mortgage/Rent: $________

Real Estate Taxes: $________

Maintenance/Repairs: $________

Association Dues: $________

Utilities

Electric/Gas: $________

Water: $________

Phone: $________

Internet: $________

Cable: $________

Other____________: $________

Food

Groceries: $________

Takeout: $________

MONTHLY BUDGET CONTINUED

Month:___________

Clothing

Adults:	$______
Kids:	$______
Cleaning/Laundry/Repairs	$______
Other___________: :	$______

Transportation

Car payment:	$______
Gas:	$______
Repairs/Maintenance:	$______
Public transportation:	$______
Other___________:	$______

Health & Medicine

Medication:	$______
Doctor Bills:	$______
Copay:	$______
Pets:	$______
Other___________:	$______

Insurances

Health Insurance:	$______
Life Insurance:	$______
Homeowner/Renter:	$______
Auto Insurance:	$______
Other policies___________:	$______

Personal

Personal Care/Grooming:	$______
Toiletries	$______
Tuition Fees:	$______
Books/Supplies:	$______
Child Care/Babysitter:	$______

MONTHLY BUDGET

Monthly Income **Month:___________**

Income (Source 1): $________

Income (Source 2): $________

Total Monthly Income: $________

Charity

Tithe/Giving: $________

Saving

Emergency Fund: $________

Retirement Fund: $________

Housing

Mortgage/Rent: $________

Real Estate Taxes: $________

Maintenance/Repairs: $________

Association Dues: $________

Utilities

Electric/Gas: $________

Water: $________

Phone: $________

Internet: $________

Cable: $________

Other____________: $________

Food

Groceries: $________

Takeout: $________

MONTHLY BUDGET CONTINUED

Month:___________

Clothing

Adults:	$______
Kids:	$______
Cleaning/Laundry/Repairs	$______
Other____________: :	$______

Transportation

Car payment:	$______
Gas:	$______
Repairs/Maintenance:	$______
Public transportation:	$______
Other____________:	$______

Health & Medicine

Medication:	$______
Doctor Bills:	$______
Copay:	$______
Pets:	$______
Other____________:	$______

Insurances

Health Insurance:	$______
Life Insurance:	$______
Homeowner/Renter:	$______
Auto Insurance:	$______
Other policies____________:	$______

Personal

Personal Care/Grooming:	$______
Toiletries	$______
Tuition Fees:	$______
Books/Supplies:	$______
Child Care/Babysitter:	$______

MONTHLY BUDGET

Monthly Income **Month:___________**

Income (Source 1): $________

Income (Source 2): $________

Total Monthly Income: $________

Charity

Tithe/Giving: $________

Saving

Emergency Fund: $________

Retirement Fund: $________

Housing

Mortgage/Rent: $________

Real Estate Taxes: $________

Maintenance/Repairs: $________

Association Dues: $________

Utilities

Electric/Gas: $________

Water: $________

Phone: $________

Internet: $________

Cable: $________

Other____________: $________

Food

Groceries: $________

Takeout: $________

MONTHLY BUDGET CONTINUED

Month:___________

Clothing

Adults: $______

Kids: $______

Cleaning/Laundry/Repairs $______

Other____________: : $______

Transportation

Car payment: $______

Gas: $______

Repairs/Maintenance: $______

Public transportation: $______

Other____________: $______

Health & Medicine

Medication: $______

Doctor Bills: $______

Copay: $______

Pets: $______

Other____________: $______

Insurances

Health Insurance: $______

Life Insurance: $______

Homeowner/Renter: $______

Auto Insurance: $______

Other policies____________: $______

Personal

Personal Care/Grooming: $______

Toiletries $______

Tuition Fees: $______

Books/Supplies: $______

Child Care/Babysitter: $______

MONTHLY BUDGET

Month:___________

Monthly Income

Income (Source 1): $_______

Income (Source 2): $_______

Total Monthly Income: $_______

Charity

Tithe/Giving: $_______

Saving

Emergency Fund: $_______

Retirement Fund: $_______

Housing

Mortgage/Rent: $_______

Real Estate Taxes: $_______

Maintenance/Repairs: $_______

Association Dues: $_______

Utilities

Electric/Gas: $_______

Water: $_______

Phone: $_______

Internet: $_______

Cable: $_______

Other____________: $_______

Food

Groceries: $_______

Takeout: $_______

MONTHLY BUDGET CONTINUED

Month:___________

Clothing

Adults:	$______
Kids:	$______
Cleaning/Laundry/Repairs	$______
Other____________: :	$______

Transportation

Car payment:	$______
Gas:	$______
Repairs/Maintenance:	$______
Public transportation:	$______
Other____________:	$______

Health & Medicine

Medication:	$______
Doctor Bills:	$______
Copay:	$______
Pets:	$______
Other____________:	$______

Insurances

Health Insurance:	$______
Life Insurance:	$______
Homeowner/Renter:	$______
Auto Insurance:	$______
Other policies_____________:	$______

Personal

Personal Care/Grooming:	$______
Toiletries	$______
Tuition Fees:	$______
Books/Supplies:	$______
Child Care/Babysitter:	$______

MONTHLY BUDGET

Month:___________

Monthly Income

Income (Source 1): $________
Income (Source 2): $________
Total Monthly Income: $________

Charity
Tithe/Giving: $________

Saving
Emergency Fund: $________
Retirement Fund: $________

Housing
Mortgage/Rent: $________
Real Estate Taxes: $________
Maintenance/Repairs: $________
Association Dues: $________

Utilities
Electric/Gas: $________
Water: $________
Phone: $________
Internet: $________
Cable: $________
Other____________: $________

Food
Groceries: $________
Takeout: $________

MONTHLY BUDGET CONTINUED

Month:___________

Clothing

Adults: $______

Kids: $______

Cleaning/Laundry/Repairs $______

Other____________: : $______

Transportation

Car payment: $______

Gas: $______

Repairs/Maintenance: $______

Public transportation: $______

Other____________: $______

Health & Medicine

Medication: $______

Doctor Bills: $______

Copay: $______

Pets: $______

Other____________: $______

Insurances

Health Insurance: $______

Life Insurance: $______

Homeowner/Renter: $______

Auto Insurance: $______

Other policies____________: $______

Personal

Personal Care/Grooming: $______

Toiletries $______

Tuition Fees: $______

Books/Supplies: $______

Child Care/Babysitter: $______

MONTHLY BUDGET

Monthly Income **Month:____________**

Income (Source 1): $________

Income (Source 2): $________

Total Monthly Income: $________

Charity

Tithe/Giving: $________

Saving

Emergency Fund: $________

Retirement Fund: $________

Housing

Mortgage/Rent: $________

Real Estate Taxes: $________

Maintenance/Repairs: $________

Association Dues: $________

Utilities

Electric/Gas: $________

Water: $________

Phone: $________

Internet: $________

Cable: $________

Other____________: $________

Food

Groceries: $________

Takeout: $________

MONTHLY BUDGET CONTINUED

Month:___________

Clothing

Adults: $______
Kids: $______
Cleaning/Laundry/Repairs $______
Other____________: : $______

Transportation

Car payment: $______
Gas: $______
Repairs/Maintenance: $______
Public transportation: $______
Other____________: $______

Health & Medicine

Medication: $______
Doctor Bills: $______
Copay: $______
Pets: $______
Other____________: $______

Insurances

Health Insurance: $______
Life Insurance: $______
Homeowner/Renter: $______
Auto Insurance: $______
Other policies____________: $______

Personal

Personal Care/Grooming: $______
Toiletries $______
Tuition Fees: $______
Books/Supplies: $______
Child Care/Babysitter: $______

MONTHLY BUDGET

Monthly Income

Month:____________

Income (Source 1): $________

Income (Source 2): $________

Total Monthly Income: $________

Charity

Tithe/Giving: $________

Saving

Emergency Fund: $________

Retirement Fund: $________

Housing

Mortgage/Rent: $________

Real Estate Taxes: $________

Maintenance/Repairs: $________

Association Dues: $________

Utilities

Electric/Gas: $________

Water: $________

Phone: $________

Internet: $________

Cable: $________

Other_____________: $________

Food

Groceries: $________

Takeout: $________

MONTHLY BUDGET CONTINUED

Month:___________

Clothing

Adults: $______

Kids: $______

Cleaning/Laundry/Repairs $______

Other____________: : $______

Transportation

Car payment: $______

Gas: $______

Repairs/Maintenance: $______

Public transportation: $______

Other____________: $______

Health & Medicine

Medication: $______

Doctor Bills: $______

Copay: $______

Pets: $______

Other____________: $______

Insurances

Health Insurance: $______

Life Insurance: $______

Homeowner/Renter: $______

Auto Insurance: $______

Other policies____________: $______

Personal

Personal Care/Grooming: $______

Toiletries $______

Tuition Fees: $______

Books/Supplies: $______

Child Care/Babysitter: $______

MONTHLY BUDGET

Monthly Income Month:___________

Income (Source 1): $_______
Income (Source 2): $_______
Total Monthly Income: $_______

Charity
Tithe/Giving: $_______

Saving
Emergency Fund: $_______
Retirement Fund: $_______

Housing
Mortgage/Rent: $_______
Real Estate Taxes: $_______
Maintenance/Repairs: $_______
Association Dues: $_______

Utilities
Electric/Gas: $_______
Water: $_______
Phone: $_______
Internet: $_______
Cable: $_______
Other____________: $_______

Food
Groceries: $_______
Takeout: $_______

MONTHLY BUDGET CONTINUED

Month:___________

Clothing

Adults: $_______
Kids: $_______
Cleaning/Laundry/Repairs $_______
Other____________: : $_______

Transportation

Car payment: $_______
Gas: $_______
Repairs/Maintenance: $_______
Public transportation: $_______
Other____________: $_______

Health & Medicine

Medication: $_______
Doctor Bills: $_______
Copay: $_______
Pets: $_______
Other____________: $_______

Insurances

Health Insurance: $_______
Life Insurance: $_______
Homeowner/Renter: $_______
Auto Insurance: $_______
Other policies____________: $_______

Personal

Personal Care/Grooming: $_______
Toiletries $_______
Tuition Fees: $_______
Books/Supplies: $_______
Child Care/Babysitter: $_______

MONTHLY BUDGET

Monthly Income **Month:____________**

Income (Source 1): $________

Income (Source 2): $________

Total Monthly Income: $________

Charity

Tithe/Giving: $________

Saving

Emergency Fund: $________

Retirement Fund: $________

Housing

Mortgage/Rent: $________

Real Estate Taxes: $________

Maintenance/Repairs: $________

Association Dues: $________

Utilities

Electric/Gas: $________

Water: $________

Phone: $________

Internet: $________

Cable: $________

Other____________: $________

Food

Groceries: $________

Takeout: $________

MONTHLY BUDGET CONTINUED

Month:___________

Clothing
Adults: $______
Kids: $______
Cleaning/Laundry/Repairs $______
Other____________: $______

Transportation $______
Car payment: $______
Gas: $______
Repairs/Maintenance: $______
Public transportation: $______
Other____________:

Health & Medicine
Medication: $______
Doctor Bills: $______
Copay: $______
Pets: $______
Other____________: $______

Insurances
Health Insurance: $______
Life Insurance: $______
Homeowner/Renter: $______
Auto Insurance: $______
Other policies_____________: $______

Personal
Personal Care/Grooming: $______
Toiletries $______
Tuition Fees: $______
Books/Supplies: $______
Child Care/Babysitter: $______

MONTHLY BUDGET

Month:___________

Monthly Income

Income (Source 1): $______

Income (Source 2): $______

Total Monthly Income: $______

Charity

Tithe/Giving: $______

Saving

Emergency Fund: $______

Retirement Fund: $______

Housing

Mortgage/Rent: $______

Real Estate Taxes: $______

Maintenance/Repairs: $______

Association Dues: $______

Utilities

Electric/Gas: $______

Water: $______

Phone: $______

Internet: $______

Cable: $______

Other____________: $______

Food

Groceries: $______

Takeout: $______

MONTHLY BUDGET CONTINUED

Month:___________

Clothing

Adults: $________
Kids: $________
Cleaning/Laundry/Repairs $________
Other____________: : $________

Transportation

Car payment: $________
Gas: $________
Repairs/Maintenance: $________
Public transportation: $________
Other____________: $________

Health & Medicine

Medication: $________
Doctor Bills: $________
Copay: $________
Pets: $________
Other____________: $________

Insurances

Health Insurance: $________
Life Insurance: $________
Homeowner/Renter: $________
Auto Insurance: $________
Other policies____________: $________

Personal

Personal Care/Grooming: $________
Toiletries $________
Tuition Fees: $________
Books/Supplies: $________
Child Care/Babysitter: $________

MONTHLY BUDGET

Month:___________

Monthly Income

Income (Source 1): $_______

Income (Source 2): $_______

Total Monthly Income: $_______

Charity

Tithe/Giving: $_______

Saving

Emergency Fund: $_______

Retirement Fund: $_______

Housing

Mortgage/Rent: $_______

Real Estate Taxes: $_______

Maintenance/Repairs: $_______

Association Dues: $_______

Utilities

Electric/Gas: $_______

Water: $_______

Phone: $_______

Internet: $_______

Cable: $_______

Other____________: $_______

Food

Groceries: $_______

Takeout: $_______

MONTHLY BUDGET CONTINUED

Month:___________

Clothing

Adults:	$______
Kids:	$______
Cleaning/Laundry/Repairs	$______
Other____________: :	$______

Transportation

Car payment:	$______
Gas:	$______
Repairs/Maintenance:	$______
Public transportation:	$______
Other____________:	$______

Health & Medicine

Medication:	$______
Doctor Bills:	$______
Copay:	$______
Pets:	$______
Other____________:	$______

Insurances

Health Insurance:	$______
Life Insurance:	$______
Homeowner/Renter:	$______
Auto Insurance:	$______
Other policies____________:	$______

Personal

Personal Care/Grooming:	$______
Toiletries	$______
Tuition Fees:	$______
Books/Supplies:	$______
Child Care/Babysitter:	$______

MONTHLY BUDGET

Monthly Income Month:___________

Income (Source 1): $_______
Income (Source 2): $_______
Total Monthly Income: $_______

Charity
Tithe/Giving: $_______

Saving
Emergency Fund: $_______
Retirement Fund: $_______

Housing
Mortgage/Rent: $_______
Real Estate Taxes: $_______
Maintenance/Repairs: $_______
Association Dues: $_______

Utilities
Electric/Gas: $_______
Water: $_______
Phone: $_______
Internet: $_______
Cable: $_______
Other____________: $_______

Food
Groceries: $_______
Takeout: $_______

MONTHLY BUDGET CONTINUED

Month:___________

Clothing

Adults: $______
Kids: $______
Cleaning/Laundry/Repairs $______
Other____________: $______

Transportation

Car payment: $______
Gas: $______
Repairs/Maintenance: $______
Public transportation: $______
Other____________: $______

Health & Medicine

Medication: $______
Doctor Bills: $______
Copay: $______
Pets: $______
Other____________: $______

Insurances

Health Insurance: $______
Life Insurance: $______
Homeowner/Renter: $______
Auto Insurance: $______
Other policies____________: $______

Personal

Personal Care/Grooming: $______
Toiletries $______
Tuition Fees: $______
Books/Supplies: $______
Child Care/Babysitter: $______

MONTHLY BUDGET

Month:___________

Monthly Income

Income (Source 1): $________
Income (Source 2): $________
Total Monthly Income: $________

Charity
Tithe/Giving: $________

Saving
Emergency Fund: $________
Retirement Fund: $________

Housing
Mortgage/Rent: $________
Real Estate Taxes: $________
Maintenance/Repairs: $________
Association Dues: $________

Utilities
Electric/Gas: $________
Water: $________
Phone: $________
Internet: $________
Cable: $________
Other____________: $________

Food
Groceries: $________
Takeout: $________

MONTHLY BUDGET CONTINUED

Month:___________

Clothing

Adults: $_______
Kids: $_______
Cleaning/Laundry/Repairs $_______
Other____________: $_______

Transportation

Car payment: $_______
Gas: $_______
Repairs/Maintenance: $_______
Public transportation: $_______
Other____________: $_______

Health & Medicine

Medication: $_______
Doctor Bills: $_______
Copay: $_______
Pets: $_______
Other____________: $_______

Insurances

Health Insurance: $_______
Life Insurance: $_______
Homeowner/Renter: $_______
Auto Insurance: $_______
Other policies____________: $_______

Personal

Personal Care/Grooming: $_______
Toiletries $_______
Tuition Fees: $_______
Books/Supplies: $_______
Child Care/Babysitter: $_______

MONTHLY BUDGET

Monthly Income Month:___________

Income (Source 1): $________

Income (Source 2): $________

Total Monthly Income: $________

Charity

Tithe/Giving: $________

Saving

Emergency Fund: $________

Retirement Fund: $________

Housing

Mortgage/Rent: $________

Real Estate Taxes: $________

Maintenance/Repairs: $________

Association Dues: $________

Utilities

Electric/Gas: $________

Water: $________

Phone: $________

Internet: $________

Cable: $________

Other____________: $________

Food

Groceries: $________

Takeout: $________

MONTHLY BUDGET CONTINUED

Month:___________

Clothing

Adults: $_______
Kids: $_______
Cleaning/Laundry/Repairs $_______
Other____________: $_______

Transportation

Car payment: $_______
Gas: $_______
Repairs/Maintenance: $_______
Public transportation: $_______
Other____________: $_______

Health & Medicine

Medication: $_______
Doctor Bills: $_______
Copay: $_______
Pets: $_______
Other____________: $_______

Insurances

Health Insurance: $_______
Life Insurance: $_______
Homeowner/Renter: $_______
Auto Insurance: $_______
Other policies_____________: $_______

Personal

Personal Care/Grooming: $_______
Toiletries $_______
Tuition Fees: $_______
Books/Supplies: $_______
Child Care/Babysitter: $_______

MONTHLY BUDGET

Monthly Income **Month:___________**

Income (Source 1): $_______

Income (Source 2): $_______

Total Monthly Income: $_______

Charity

Tithe/Giving: $_______

Saving

Emergency Fund: $_______

Retirement Fund: $_______

Housing

Mortgage/Rent: $_______

Real Estate Taxes: $_______

Maintenance/Repairs: $_______

Association Dues: $_______

Utilities

Electric/Gas: $_______

Water: $_______

Phone: $_______

Internet: $_______

Cable: $_______

Other____________: $_______

Food

Groceries: $_______

Takeout: $_______

MONTHLY BUDGET CONTINUED

Month:___________

Clothing

Adults:	$_______
Kids:	$_______
Cleaning/Laundry/Repairs	$_______
Other____________:	$_______

Transportation

Car payment:	$_______
Gas:	$_______
Repairs/Maintenance:	$_______
Public transportation:	$_______
Other____________:	$_______

Health & Medicine

Medication:	$_______
Doctor Bills:	$_______
Copay:	$_______
Pets:	$_______
Other____________:	$_______

Insurances

Health Insurance:	$_______
Life Insurance:	$_______
Homeowner/Renter:	$_______
Auto Insurance:	$_______
Other policies____________:	$_______

Personal

Personal Care/Grooming:	$_______
Toiletries	$_______
Tuition Fees:	$_______
Books/Supplies:	$_______
Child Care/Babysitter:	$_______

MONTHLY BUDGET

Monthly Income Month:___________

Income (Source 1): $________
Income (Source 2): $________
Total Monthly Income: $________

Charity
Tithe/Giving: $________

Saving
Emergency Fund: $________
Retirement Fund: $________

Housing
Mortgage/Rent: $________
Real Estate Taxes: $________
Maintenance/Repairs: $________
Association Dues: $________

Utilities
Electric/Gas: $________
Water: $________
Phone: $________
Internet: $________
Cable: $________
Other____________: $________

Food
Groceries: $________
Takeout: $________

MONTHLY BUDGET CONTINUED

Month:___________

Clothing

Adults: $_______

Kids: $_______

Cleaning/Laundry/Repairs $_______

Other____________: : $_______

Transportation

Car payment: $_______

Gas: $_______

Repairs/Maintenance: $_______

Public transportation: $_______

Other____________: $_______

Health & Medicine

Medication: $_______

Doctor Bills: $_______

Copay: $_______

Pets: $_______

Other____________: $_______

Insurances

Health Insurance: $_______

Life Insurance: $_______

Homeowner/Renter: $_______

Auto Insurance: $_______

Other policies____________: $_______

Personal

Personal Care/Grooming: $_______

Toiletries $_______

Tuition Fees: $_______

Books/Supplies: $_______

Child Care/Babysitter: $_______

MONTHLY BUDGET

Month:___________

Monthly Income

Income (Source 1):	$_______
Income (Source 2):	$_______
Total Monthly Income:	$_______

Charity

Tithe/Giving:	$_______

Saving

Emergency Fund:	$_______
Retirement Fund:	$_______

Housing

Mortgage/Rent:	$_______
Real Estate Taxes:	$_______
Maintenance/Repairs:	$_______
Association Dues:	$_______

Utilities

Electric/Gas:	$_______
Water:	$_______
Phone:	$_______
Internet:	$_______
Cable:	$_______
Other____________:	$_______

Food

Groceries:	$_______
Takeout:	$_______

MONTHLY BUDGET CONTINUED

Month:___________

Clothing

Adults: $_______
Kids: $_______
Cleaning/Laundry/Repairs $_______
Other____________: : $_______

Transportation

Car payment: $_______
Gas: $_______
Repairs/Maintenance: $_______
Public transportation: $_______
Other____________: $_______

Health & Medicine

Medication: $_______
Doctor Bills: $_______
Copay: $_______
Pets: $_______
Other____________: $_______

Insurances

Health Insurance: $_______
Life Insurance: $_______
Homeowner/Renter: $_______
Auto Insurance: $_______
Other policies____________: $_______

Personal

Personal Care/Grooming: $_______
Toiletries $_______
Tuition Fees: $_______
Books/Supplies: $_______
Child Care/Babysitter: $_______

MONTHLY BUDGET

Monthly Income Month:___________

Income (Source 1): $________

Income (Source 2): $________

Total Monthly Income: $________

Charity

Tithe/Giving: $________

Saving

Emergency Fund: $________

Retirement Fund: $________

Housing

Mortgage/Rent: $________

Real Estate Taxes: $________

Maintenance/Repairs: $________

Association Dues: $________

Utilities

Electric/Gas: $________

Water: $________

Phone: $________

Internet: $________

Cable: $________

Other____________: $________

Food

Groceries: $________

Takeout: $________

MONTHLY BUDGET CONTINUED

Month:___________

Clothing

Adults: $_______
Kids: $_______
Cleaning/Laundry/Repairs $_______
Other____________: $_______

Transportation

Car payment: $_______
Gas: $_______
Repairs/Maintenance: $_______
Public transportation: $_______
Other____________: $_______

Health & Medicine

Medication: $_______
Doctor Bills: $_______
Copay: $_______
Pets: $_______
Other____________: $_______

Insurances

Health Insurance: $_______
Life Insurance: $_______
Homeowner/Renter: $_______
Auto Insurance: $_______
Other policies____________: $_______

Personal

Personal Care/Grooming: $_______
Toiletries $_______
Tuition Fees: $_______
Books/Supplies: $_______
Child Care/Babysitter: $_______

MONTHLY BUDGET

Monthly Income **Month:____________**

Income (Source 1): $________

Income (Source 2): $________

Total Monthly Income: $________

Charity

Tithe/Giving: $________

Saving

Emergency Fund: $________

Retirement Fund: $________

Housing

Mortgage/Rent: $________

Real Estate Taxes: $________

Maintenance/Repairs: $________

Association Dues: $________

Utilities

Electric/Gas: $________

Water: $________

Phone: $________

Internet: $________

Cable: $________

Other____________: $________

Food

Groceries: $________

Takeout: $________

MONTHLY BUDGET CONTINUED

Month:___________

Clothing

Adults: $_______

Kids: $_______

Cleaning/Laundry/Repairs $_______

Other____________: $_______

Transportation

Car payment: $_______

Gas: $_______

Repairs/Maintenance: $_______

Public transportation: $_______

Other____________: $_______

Health & Medicine

Medication: $_______

Doctor Bills: $_______

Copay: $_______

Pets: $_______

Other____________: $_______

Insurances

Health Insurance: $_______

Life Insurance: $_______

Homeowner/Renter: $_______

Auto Insurance: $_______

Other policies_____________: $_______

Personal

Personal Care/Grooming: $_______

Toiletries $_______

Tuition Fees: $_______

Books/Supplies: $_______

Child Care/Babysitter: $_______

MONTHLY BUDGET

Month:____________

Monthly Income

Income (Source 1): $________

Income (Source 2): $________

Total Monthly Income: $________

Charity

Tithe/Giving: $________

Saving

Emergency Fund: $________

Retirement Fund: $________

Housing

Mortgage/Rent: $________

Real Estate Taxes: $________

Maintenance/Repairs: $________

Association Dues: $________

Utilities

Electric/Gas: $________

Water: $________

Phone: $________

Internet: $________

Cable: $________

Other______________: $________

Food

Groceries: $________

Takeout: $________

MONTHLY BUDGET CONTINUED

Month:___________

Clothing

Adults: $______
Kids: $______
Cleaning/Laundry/Repairs $______
Other____________: : $______

Transportation

Car payment: $______
Gas: $______
Repairs/Maintenance: $______
Public transportation: $______
Other____________: $______

Health & Medicine

Medication: $______
Doctor Bills: $______
Copay: $______
Pets: $______
Other____________: $______

Insurances

Health Insurance: $______
Life Insurance: $______
Homeowner/Renter: $______
Auto Insurance: $______
Other policies_____________: $______

Personal

Personal Care/Grooming: $______
Toiletries $______
Tuition Fees: $______
Books/Supplies: $______
Child Care/Babysitter: $______

MONTHLY BUDGET

Month:___________

Monthly Income

Income (Source 1): $________

Income (Source 2): $________

Total Monthly Income: $________

Charity

Tithe/Giving: $________

Saving

Emergency Fund: $________

Retirement Fund: $________

Housing $________

Mortgage/Rent:

Real Estate Taxes: $________

Maintenance/Repairs: $________

Association Dues: $________

Utilities

Electric/Gas: $________

Water: $________

Phone: $________

Internet: $________

Cable: $________

Other____________: $________

Food

Groceries: $________

Takeout: $________

MONTHLY BUDGET CONTINUED

Month:___________

Clothing

Adults: $_______

Kids: $_______

Cleaning/Laundry/Repairs $_______

Other____________: : $_______

Transportation

Car payment: $_______

Gas: $_______

Repairs/Maintenance: $_______

Public transportation: $_______

Other____________: $_______

Health & Medicine

Medication: $_______

Doctor Bills: $_______

Copay: $_______

Pets: $_______

Other____________: $_______

Insurances

Health Insurance: $_______

Life Insurance: $_______

Homeowner/Renter: $_______

Auto Insurance: $_______

Other policies____________: $_______

Personal

Personal Care/Grooming: $_______

Toiletries $_______

Tuition Fees: $_______

Books/Supplies: $_______

Child Care/Babysitter: $_______

MONTHLY BUDGET

Monthly Income **Month:___________**

Income (Source 1): $________
Income (Source 2): $________
Total Monthly Income: $________

Charity
Tithe/Giving: $________

Saving
Emergency Fund: $________
Retirement Fund: $________

Housing
Mortgage/Rent: $________
Real Estate Taxes: $________
Maintenance/Repairs: $________
Association Dues: $________

Utilities
Electric/Gas: $________
Water: $________
Phone: $________
Internet: $________
Cable: $________
Other____________: $________

Food
Groceries: $________
Takeout: $________

MONTHLY BUDGET CONTINUED

Month:___________

Clothing

Adults: $______

Kids: $______

Cleaning/Laundry/Repairs $______

Other____________: $______

Transportation

Car payment: $______

Gas: $______

Repairs/Maintenance: $______

Public transportation: $______

Other____________: $______

Health & Medicine

Medication: $______

Doctor Bills: $______

Copay: $______

Pets: $______

Other____________: $______

Insurances

Health Insurance: $______

Life Insurance: $______

Homeowner/Renter: $______

Auto Insurance: $______

Other policies____________: $______

Personal

Personal Care/Grooming: $______

Toiletries $______

Tuition Fees: $______

Books/Supplies: $______

Child Care/Babysitter: $______

MONTHLY BUDGET

Month:___________

Monthly Income

Income (Source 1): $________
Income (Source 2): $________
Total Monthly Income: $________

Charity
Tithe/Giving: $________

Saving
Emergency Fund: $________
Retirement Fund: $________

Housing
Mortgage/Rent: $________
Real Estate Taxes: $________
Maintenance/Repairs: $________
Association Dues: $________

Utilities
Electric/Gas: $________
Water: $________
Phone: $________
Internet: $________
Cable: $________
Other____________: $________

Food
Groceries: $________
Takeout: $________

MONTHLY BUDGET CONTINUED

Month:___________

Clothing

Adults: $_______

Kids: $_______

Cleaning/Laundry/Repairs $_______

Other____________: $_______

Transportation

Car payment: $_______

Gas: $_______

Repairs/Maintenance: $_______

Public transportation: $_______

Other____________: $_______

Health & Medicine

Medication: $_______

Doctor Bills: $_______

Copay: $_______

Pets: $_______

Other____________: $_______

Insurances

Health Insurance: $_______

Life Insurance: $_______

Homeowner/Renter: $_______

Auto Insurance: $_______

Other policies____________: $_______

Personal

Personal Care/Grooming: $_______

Toiletries $_______

Tuition Fees: $_______

Books/Supplies: $_______

Child Care/Babysitter: $_______

MONTHLY BUDGET

Monthly Income **Month:___________**

Income (Source 1): $_______
Income (Source 2): $_______
Total Monthly Income: $_______

Charity
Tithe/Giving: $_______

Saving
Emergency Fund: $_______
Retirement Fund: $_______

Housing
Mortgage/Rent: $_______
Real Estate Taxes: $_______
Maintenance/Repairs: $_______
Association Dues: $_______

Utilities
Electric/Gas: $_______
Water: $_______
Phone: $_______
Internet: $_______
Cable: $_______
Other____________: $_______

Food
Groceries: $_______
Takeout: $_______

MONTHLY BUDGET CONTINUED

Month:___________

Clothing

Adults: $_______
Kids: $_______
Cleaning/Laundry/Repairs $_______
Other____________: : $_______

Transportation

Car payment: $_______
Gas: $_______
Repairs/Maintenance: $_______
Public transportation: $_______
Other____________: $_______

Health & Medicine

Medication: $_______
Doctor Bills: $_______
Copay: $_______
Pets: $_______
Other____________: $_______

Insurances

Health Insurance: $_______
Life Insurance: $_______
Homeowner/Renter: $_______
Auto Insurance: $_______
Other policies____________: $_______

Personal

Personal Care/Grooming: $_______
Toiletries $_______
Tuition Fees: $_______
Books/Supplies: $_______
Child Care/Babysitter: $_______

MONTHLY BUDGET

Month:___________

Monthly Income

Income (Source 1):	$_______
Income (Source 2):	$_______
Total Monthly Income:	$_______
Charity	
Tithe/Giving:	$_______
Saving	
Emergency Fund:	$_______
Retirement Fund:	$_______
Housing	
Mortgage/Rent:	$_______
Real Estate Taxes:	$_______
Maintenance/Repairs:	$_______
Association Dues:	$_______
Utilities	
Electric/Gas:	$_______
Water:	$_______
Phone:	$_______
Internet:	$_______
Cable:	$_______
Other____________:	$_______
Food	
Groceries:	$_______
Takeout:	$_______

MONTHLY BUDGET CONTINUED

Month:___________

Clothing

Adults:	$______
Kids:	$______
Cleaning/Laundry/Repairs	$______
Other____________: :	$______

Transportation

Car payment:	$______
Gas:	$______
Repairs/Maintenance:	$______
Public transportation:	$______
Other____________:	$______

Health & Medicine

Medication:	$______
Doctor Bills:	$______
Copay:	$______
Pets:	$______
Other____________:	$______

Insurances

Health Insurance:	$______
Life Insurance:	$______
Homeowner/Renter:	$______
Auto Insurance:	$______
Other policies____________:	$______

Personal

Personal Care/Grooming:	$______
Toiletries	$______
Tuition Fees:	$______
Books/Supplies:	$______
Child Care/Babysitter:	$______

MONTHLY BUDGET

Month:___________

Monthly Income

Income (Source 1): $______

Income (Source 2): $______

Total Monthly Income: $______

Charity

Tithe/Giving: $______

Saving

Emergency Fund: $______

Retirement Fund: $______

Housing

Mortgage/Rent: $______

Real Estate Taxes: $______

Maintenance/Repairs: $______

Association Dues: $______

Utilities

Electric/Gas: $______

Water: $______

Phone: $______

Internet: $______

Cable: $______

Other___________: $______

Food

Groceries: $______

Takeout: $______

MONTHLY BUDGET CONTINUED

Month:___________

Clothing

Adults:	$_______
Kids:	$_______
Cleaning/Laundry/Repairs	$_______
Other____________:	$_______

Transportation

Car payment:	$_______
Gas:	$_______
Repairs/Maintenance:	$_______
Public transportation:	$_______
Other____________:	$_______

Health & Medicine

Medication:	$_______
Doctor Bills:	$_______
Copay:	$_______
Pets:	$_______
Other____________:	$_______

Insurances

Health Insurance:	$_______
Life Insurance:	$_______
Homeowner/Renter:	$_______
Auto Insurance:	$_______
Other policies____________:	$_______

Personal

Personal Care/Grooming:	$_______
Toiletries	$_______
Tuition Fees:	$_______
Books/Supplies:	$_______
Child Care/Babysitter:	$_______

MONTHLY BUDGET

Monthly Income **Month:___________**

Income (Source 1): $________

Income (Source 2): $________

Total Monthly Income: $________

Charity

Tithe/Giving: $________

Saving

Emergency Fund: $________

Retirement Fund: $________

Housing

Mortgage/Rent: $________

Real Estate Taxes: $________

Maintenance/Repairs: $________

Association Dues: $________

Utilities

Electric/Gas: $________

Water: $________

Phone: $________

Internet: $________

Cable: $________

Other____________: $________

Food

Groceries: $________

Takeout: $________

MONTHLY BUDGET CONTINUED

Month:___________

Clothing

Adults: $_______
Kids: $_______
Cleaning/Laundry/Repairs $_______
Other____________: $_______

Transportation

Car payment: $_______
Gas: $_______
Repairs/Maintenance: $_______
Public transportation: $_______
Other____________: $_______

Health & Medicine

Medication: $_______
Doctor Bills: $_______
Copay: $_______
Pets: $_______
Other____________: $_______

Insurances

Health Insurance: $_______
Life Insurance: $_______
Homeowner/Renter: $_______
Auto Insurance: $_______
Other policies____________: $_______

Personal

Personal Care/Grooming: $_______
Toiletries $_______
Tuition Fees: $_______
Books/Supplies: $_______
Child Care/Babysitter: $_______

MONTHLY BUDGET

Month:___________

Monthly Income

Income (Source 1): $_______

Income (Source 2): $_______

Total Monthly Income: $_______

Charity

Tithe/Giving: $_______

Saving

Emergency Fund: $_______

Retirement Fund: $_______

Housing

Mortgage/Rent: $_______

Real Estate Taxes: $_______

Maintenance/Repairs: $_______

Association Dues: $_______

Utilities

Electric/Gas: $_______

Water: $_______

Phone: $_______

Internet: $_______

Cable: $_______

Other____________: $_______

Food

Groceries: $_______

Takeout: $_______

MONTHLY BUDGET CONTINUED

Month:___________

Clothing

Adults: $________
Kids: $________
Cleaning/Laundry/Repairs $________
Other____________: $________

Transportation

Car payment: $________
Gas: $________
Repairs/Maintenance: $________
Public transportation: $________
Other____________: $________

Health & Medicine

Medication: $________
Doctor Bills: $________
Copay: $________
Pets: $________
Other____________: $________

Insurances

Health Insurance: $________
Life Insurance: $________
Homeowner/Renter: $________
Auto Insurance: $________
Other policies____________: $________

Personal

Personal Care/Grooming: $________
Toiletries $________
Tuition Fees: $________
Books/Supplies: $________
Child Care/Babysitter: $________

MONTHLY BUDGET

Monthly Income **Month:___________**

Income (Source 1): $_______

Income (Source 2): $_______

Total Monthly Income: $_______

Charity

Tithe/Giving: $_______

Saving

Emergency Fund: $_______

Retirement Fund: $_______

Housing

Mortgage/Rent: $_______

Real Estate Taxes: $_______

Maintenance/Repairs: $_______

Association Dues: $_______

Utilities

Electric/Gas: $_______

Water: $_______

Phone: $_______

Internet: $_______

Cable: $_______

Other____________: $_______

Food

Groceries: $_______

Takeout: $_______

MONTHLY BUDGET CONTINUED

Month:___________

Clothing

Adults: $_______

Kids: $_______

Cleaning/Laundry/Repairs $_______

Other____________: $_______

Transportation

Car payment: $_______

Gas: $_______

Repairs/Maintenance: $_______

Public transportation: $_______

Other____________: $_______

Health & Medicine

Medication: $_______

Doctor Bills: $_______

Copay: $_______

Pets: $_______

Other____________: $_______

Insurances

Health Insurance: $_______

Life Insurance: $_______

Homeowner/Renter: $_______

Auto Insurance: $_______

Other policies_____________: $_______

Personal

Personal Care/Grooming: $_______

Toiletries $_______

Tuition Fees: $_______

Books/Supplies: $_______

Child Care/Babysitter: $_______

MONTHLY BUDGET

Monthly Income **Month:___________**

Income (Source 1): $_______

Income (Source 2): $_______

Total Monthly Income: $_______

Charity

Tithe/Giving: $_______

Saving

Emergency Fund: $_______

Retirement Fund: $_______

Housing

Mortgage/Rent: $_______

Real Estate Taxes: $_______

Maintenance/Repairs: $_______

Association Dues: $_______

Utilities

Electric/Gas: $_______

Water: $_______

Phone: $_______

Internet: $_______

Cable: $_______

Other____________: $_______

Food

Groceries: $_______

Takeout: $_______

MONTHLY BUDGET CONTINUED

Month:___________

Clothing

Adults: $______
Kids: $______
Cleaning/Laundry/Repairs $______
Other____________: $______

Transportation

Car payment: $______
Gas: $______
Repairs/Maintenance: $______
Public transportation: $______
Other____________: $______

Health & Medicine

Medication: $______
Doctor Bills: $______
Copay: $______
Pets: $______
Other____________: $______

Insurances

Health Insurance: $______
Life Insurance: $______
Homeowner/Renter: $______
Auto Insurance: $______
Other policies____________: $______

Personal

Personal Care/Grooming: $______
Toiletries $______
Tuition Fees: $______
Books/Supplies: $______
Child Care/Babysitter: $______

MONTHLY BUDGET

Month:___________

Monthly Income

Income (Source 1): $________
Income (Source 2): $________
Total Monthly Income: $________

Charity
Tithe/Giving: $________

Saving
Emergency Fund: $________
Retirement Fund: $________

Housing
Mortgage/Rent: $________
Real Estate Taxes: $________
Maintenance/Repairs: $________
Association Dues: $________

Utilities
Electric/Gas: $________
Water: $________
Phone: $________
Internet: $________
Cable: $________
Other____________: $________

Food
Groceries: $________
Takeout: $________

MONTHLY BUDGET CONTINUED

Month:___________

Clothing

Adults:	$_______
Kids:	$_______
Cleaning/Laundry/Repairs	$_______
Other_____________:	$_______

Transportation

Car payment:	$_______
Gas:	$_______
Repairs/Maintenance:	$_______
Public transportation:	$_______
Other_____________:	$_______

Health & Medicine

Medication:	$_______
Doctor Bills:	$_______
Copay:	$_______
Pets:	$_______
Other_____________:	$_______

Insurances

Health Insurance:	$_______
Life Insurance:	$_______
Homeowner/Renter:	$_______
Auto Insurance:	$_______
Other policies_____________:	$_______

Personal

Personal Care/Grooming:	$_______
Toiletries	$_______
Tuition Fees:	$_______
Books/Supplies:	$_______
Child Care/Babysitter:	$_______

MONTHLY BUDGET

Month:___________

Monthly Income

Income (Source 1): $________

Income (Source 2): $________

Total Monthly Income: $________

Charity

Tithe/Giving: $________

Saving

Emergency Fund: $________

Retirement Fund: $________

Housing

Mortgage/Rent: $________

Real Estate Taxes: $________

Maintenance/Repairs: $________

Association Dues: $________

Utilities

Electric/Gas: $________

Water: $________

Phone: $________

Internet: $________

Cable: $________

Other____________: $________

Food

Groceries: $________

Takeout: $________

MONTHLY BUDGET CONTINUED

Month:___________

Clothing

Adults:	$_______
Kids:	$_______
Cleaning/Laundry/Repairs	$_______
Other____________:	$_______

Transportation

Car payment:	$_______
Gas:	$_______
Repairs/Maintenance:	$_______
Public transportation:	$_______
Other____________:	$_______

Health & Medicine

Medication:	$_______
Doctor Bills:	$_______
Copay:	$_______
Pets:	$_______
Other____________:	$_______

Insurances

Health Insurance:	$_______
Life Insurance:	$_______
Homeowner/Renter:	$_______
Auto Insurance:	$_______
Other policies____________:	$_______

Personal

Personal Care/Grooming:	$_______
Toiletries	$_______
Tuition Fees:	$_______
Books/Supplies:	$_______
Child Care/Babysitter:	$_______

MONTHLY BUDGET

Monthly Income **Month:____________**

Income (Source 1): $________
Income (Source 2): $________
Total Monthly Income: $________

Charity
Tithe/Giving: $________

Saving
Emergency Fund: $________
Retirement Fund: $________

Housing
Mortgage/Rent: $________
Real Estate Taxes: $________
Maintenance/Repairs: $________
Association Dues: $________

Utilities
Electric/Gas: $________
Water: $________
Phone: $________
Internet: $________
Cable: $________
Other____________: $________

Food
Groceries: $________
Takeout: $________

MONTHLY BUDGET CONTINUED

Month:___________

Clothing

Adults: $_______

Kids: $_______

Cleaning/Laundry/Repairs $_______

Other____________: : $_______

Transportation

Car payment: $_______

Gas: $_______

Repairs/Maintenance: $_______

Public transportation: $_______

Other____________: $_______

Health & Medicine

Medication: $_______

Doctor Bills: $_______

Copay: $_______

Pets: $_______

Other____________: $_______

Insurances

Health Insurance: $_______

Life Insurance: $_______

Homeowner/Renter: $_______

Auto Insurance: $_______

Other policies____________: $_______

Personal

Personal Care/Grooming: $_______

Toiletries $_______

Tuition Fees: $_______

Books/Supplies: $_______

Child Care/Babysitter: $_______

MONTHLY BUDGET

Month:___________

Monthly Income

Income (Source 1): $_______

Income (Source 2): $_______

Total Monthly Income: $_______

Charity

Tithe/Giving: $_______

Saving

Emergency Fund: $_______

Retirement Fund: $_______

Housing

Mortgage/Rent: $_______

Real Estate Taxes: $_______

Maintenance/Repairs: $_______

Association Dues: $_______

Utilities

Electric/Gas: $_______

Water: $_______

Phone: $_______

Internet: $_______

Cable: $_______

Other____________: $_______

Food

Groceries: $_______

Takeout: $_______

MONTHLY BUDGET CONTINUED

Month:___________

Clothing

Adults:	$______
Kids:	$______
Cleaning/Laundry/Repairs	$______
Other__________:	$______

Transportation

Car payment:	$______
Gas:	$______
Repairs/Maintenance:	$______
Public transportation:	$______
Other__________:	$______

Health & Medicine

Medication:	$______
Doctor Bills:	$______
Copay:	$______
Pets:	$______
Other__________:	$______

Insurances

Health Insurance:	$______
Life Insurance:	$______
Homeowner/Renter:	$______
Auto Insurance:	$______
Other policies__________:	$______

Personal

Personal Care/Grooming:	$______
Toiletries	$______
Tuition Fees:	$______
Books/Supplies:	$______
Child Care/Babysitter:	$______

MONTHLY BUDGET

Month:___________

Monthly Income

Income (Source 1): $_______

Income (Source 2): $_______

Total Monthly Income: $_______

Charity

Tithe/Giving: $_______

Saving

Emergency Fund: $_______

Retirement Fund: $_______

Housing

Mortgage/Rent: $_______

Real Estate Taxes: $_______

Maintenance/Repairs: $_______

Association Dues: $_______

Utilities

Electric/Gas: $_______

Water: $_______

Phone: $_______

Internet: $_______

Cable: $_______

Other___________: $_______

Food

Groceries: $_______

Takeout: $_______

MONTHLY BUDGET CONTINUED

Month:___________

Clothing

Adults: $_______

Kids: $_______

Cleaning/Laundry/Repairs $_______

Other____________: $_______

Transportation

Car payment: $_______

Gas: $_______

Repairs/Maintenance: $_______

Public transportation: $_______

Other____________: $_______

Health & Medicine

Medication: $_______

Doctor Bills: $_______

Copay: $_______

Pets: $_______

Other____________: $_______

Insurances

Health Insurance: $_______

Life Insurance: $_______

Homeowner/Renter: $_______

Auto Insurance: $_______

Other policies____________: $_______

Personal

Personal Care/Grooming: $_______

Toiletries $_______

Tuition Fees: $_______

Books/Supplies: $_______

Child Care/Babysitter: $_______

MONTHLY BUDGET

Monthly Income **Month:___________**

Income (Source 1): $_______

Income (Source 2): $_______

Total Monthly Income: $_______

Charity

Tithe/Giving: $_______

Saving

Emergency Fund: $_______

Retirement Fund: $_______

Housing

Mortgage/Rent: $_______

Real Estate Taxes: $_______

Maintenance/Repairs: $_______

Association Dues: $_______

Utilities

Electric/Gas: $_______

Water: $_______

Phone: $_______

Internet: $_______

Cable: $_______

Other____________: $_______

Food

Groceries: $_______

Takeout: $_______

MONTHLY BUDGET CONTINUED

Month:___________

Clothing

Adults: $________
Kids: $________
Cleaning/Laundry/Repairs $________
Other____________: $________

Transportation

Car payment: $________
Gas: $________
Repairs/Maintenance: $________
Public transportation: $________
Other____________: $________

Health & Medicine

Medication: $________
Doctor Bills: $________
Copay: $________
Pets: $________
Other____________: $________

Insurances

Health Insurance: $________
Life Insurance: $________
Homeowner/Renter: $________
Auto Insurance: $________
Other policies____________: $________

Personal

Personal Care/Grooming: $________
Toiletries $________
Tuition Fees: $________
Books/Supplies: $________
Child Care/Babysitter: $________

MONTHLY BUDGET

Monthly Income **Month:___________**

Income (Source 1): $_______

Income (Source 2): $_______

Total Monthly Income: $_______

Charity

Tithe/Giving: $_______

Saving

Emergency Fund: $_______

Retirement Fund: $_______

Housing

Mortgage/Rent: $_______

Real Estate Taxes: $_______

Maintenance/Repairs: $_______

Association Dues: $_______

Utilities

Electric/Gas: $_______

Water: $_______

Phone: $_______

Internet: $_______

Cable: $_______

Other____________: $_______

Food

Groceries: $_______

Takeout: $_______

MONTHLY BUDGET CONTINUED

Month:___________

Clothing

Adults: $_______

Kids: $_______

Cleaning/Laundry/Repairs $_______

Other____________: $_______

Transportation

Car payment: $_______

Gas: $_______

Repairs/Maintenance: $_______

Public transportation: $_______

Other____________: $_______

Health & Medicine

Medication: $_______

Doctor Bills: $_______

Copay: $_______

Pets: $_______

Other____________: $_______

Insurances

Health Insurance: $_______

Life Insurance: $_______

Homeowner/Renter: $_______

Auto Insurance: $_______

Other policies_____________: $_______

Personal

Personal Care/Grooming: $_______

Toiletries $_______

Tuition Fees: $_______

Books/Supplies: $_______

Child Care/Babysitter: $_______

MONTHLY BUDGET

Monthly Income Month:___________

Income (Source 1): $________
Income (Source 2): $________
Total Monthly Income: $________

Charity
Tithe/Giving: $________

Saving
Emergency Fund: $________
Retirement Fund: $________

Housing
Mortgage/Rent: $________
Real Estate Taxes: $________
Maintenance/Repairs: $________
Association Dues: $________

Utilities
Electric/Gas: $________
Water: $________
Phone: $________
Internet: $________
Cable: $________
Other____________: $________

Food
Groceries: $________
Takeout: $________

MONTHLY BUDGET CONTINUED

Month:___________

Clothing

Adults: $______
Kids: $______
Cleaning/Laundry/Repairs $______
Other____________: : $______

Transportation

Car payment: $______
Gas: $______
Repairs/Maintenance: $______
Public transportation: $______
Other____________: $______

Health & Medicine

Medication: $______
Doctor Bills: $______
Copay: $______
Pets: $______
Other____________: $______

Insurances

Health Insurance: $______
Life Insurance: $______
Homeowner/Renter: $______
Auto Insurance: $______
Other policies____________: $______

Personal

Personal Care/Grooming: $______
Toiletries $______
Tuition Fees: $______
Books/Supplies: $______
Child Care/Babysitter: $______

MONTHLY BUDGET

Monthly Income Month:___________

Income (Source 1): $_______

Income (Source 2): $_______

Total Monthly Income: $_______

Charity

Tithe/Giving: $_______

Saving

Emergency Fund: $_______

Retirement Fund: $_______

Housing

Mortgage/Rent: $_______

Real Estate Taxes: $_______

Maintenance/Repairs: $_______

Association Dues: $_______

Utilities

Electric/Gas: $_______

Water: $_______

Phone: $_______

Internet: $_______

Cable: $_______

Other___________: $_______

Food

Groceries: $_______

Takeout: $_______

MONTHLY BUDGET CONTINUED

Month:___________

Clothing

Adults:	$______
Kids:	$______
Cleaning/Laundry/Repairs :	$______
Other____________:	$______

Transportation

Car payment:	$______
Gas:	$______
Repairs/Maintenance:	$______
Public transportation:	$______
Other____________:	$______

Health & Medicine

Medication:	$______
Doctor Bills:	$______
Copay:	$______
Pets:	$______
Other____________:	$______

Insurances

Health Insurance:	$______
Life Insurance:	$______
Homeowner/Renter:	$______
Auto Insurance:	$______
Other policies____________:	$______

Personal

Personal Care/Grooming:	$______
Toiletries	$______
Tuition Fees:	$______
Books/Supplies:	$______
Child Care/Babysitter:	$______

MONTHLY BUDGET

Monthly Income Month:___________

Income (Source 1): $________
Income (Source 2): $________
Total Monthly Income: $________

Charity
Tithe/Giving: $________

Saving
Emergency Fund: $________
Retirement Fund: $________

Housing
Mortgage/Rent: $________
Real Estate Taxes: $________
Maintenance/Repairs: $________
Association Dues: $________

Utilities
Electric/Gas: $________
Water: $________
Phone: $________
Internet: $________
Cable: $________
Other____________: $________

Food
Groceries: $________
Takeout: $________

MONTHLY BUDGET CONTINUED

Month:____________

Clothing	
Adults:	$_______
Kids:	$_______
Cleaning/Laundry/Repairs	$_______
Other____________: :	$_______
Transportation	
Car payment:	$_______
Gas:	$_______
Repairs/Maintenance:	$_______
Public transportation:	$_______
Other____________:	$_______
Health & Medicine	
Medication:	$_______
Doctor Bills:	$_______
Copay:	$_______
Pets:	$_______
Other____________:	$_______
Insurances	
Health Insurance:	$_______
Life Insurance:	$_______
Homeowner/Renter:	$_______
Auto Insurance:	$_______
Other policies____________:	$_______
Personal	
Personal Care/Grooming:	$_______
Toiletries	$_______
Tuition Fees:	$_______
Books/Supplies:	$_______
Child Care/Babysitter:	$_______

MONTHLY BUDGET

Month:___________

Monthly Income

Income (Source 1): $_______

Income (Source 2): $_______

Total Monthly Income: $_______

Charity

Tithe/Giving: $_______

Saving

Emergency Fund: $_______

Retirement Fund: $_______

Housing

Mortgage/Rent: $_______

Real Estate Taxes: $_______

Maintenance/Repairs: $_______

Association Dues: $_______

Utilities

Electric/Gas: $_______

Water: $_______

Phone: $_______

Internet: $_______

Cable: $_______

Other___________: $_______

Food

Groceries: $_______

Takeout: $_______

MONTHLY BUDGET CONTINUED

Month:___________

Clothing

Adults: $______

Kids: $______

Cleaning/Laundry/Repairs $______

Other____________: : $______

Transportation

Car payment: $______

Gas: $______

Repairs/Maintenance: $______

Public transportation: $______

Other____________: $______

Health & Medicine

Medication: $______

Doctor Bills: $______

Copay: $______

Pets: $______

Other____________: $______

Insurances

Health Insurance: $______

Life Insurance: $______

Homeowner/Renter: $______

Auto Insurance: $______

Other policies____________: $______

Personal

Personal Care/Grooming: $______

Toiletries $______

Tuition Fees: $______

Books/Supplies: $______

Child Care/Babysitter: $______

MONTHLY BUDGET

Month:___________

Monthly Income

Income (Source 1): $________

Income (Source 2): $________

Total Monthly Income: $________

Charity

Tithe/Giving: $________

Saving

Emergency Fund: $________

Retirement Fund: $________

Housing $________

Mortgage/Rent:

Real Estate Taxes: $________

Maintenance/Repairs: $________

Association Dues: $________

Utilities

Electric/Gas: $________

Water: $________

Phone: $________

Internet: $________

Cable: $________

Other____________: $________

Food

Groceries: $________

Takeout: $________

MONTHLY BUDGET CONTINUED

Month:___________

Clothing

Adults: $_______

Kids: $_______

Cleaning/Laundry/Repairs $_______

Other____________: : $_______

Transportation

Car payment: $_______

Gas: $_______

Repairs/Maintenance: $_______

Public transportation: $_______

Other____________: $_______

Health & Medicine

Medication: $_______

Doctor Bills: $_______

Copay: $_______

Pets: $_______

Other____________: $_______

Insurances

Health Insurance: $_______

Life Insurance: $_______

Homeowner/Renter: $_______

Auto Insurance: $_______

Other policies____________: $_______

Personal

Personal Care/Grooming: $_______

Toiletries $_______

Tuition Fees: $_______

Books/Supplies: $_______

Child Care/Babysitter: $_______

MONTHLY BUDGET

Monthly Income **Month:___________**

Income (Source 1): $________
Income (Source 2): $________
Total Monthly Income: $________

Charity
Tithe/Giving: $________

Saving
Emergency Fund: $________
Retirement Fund: $________

Housing
Mortgage/Rent: $________
Real Estate Taxes: $________
Maintenance/Repairs: $________
Association Dues: $________

Utilities
Electric/Gas: $________
Water: $________
Phone: $________
Internet: $________
Cable: $________
Other____________: $________

Food
Groceries: $________
Takeout: $________

MONTHLY BUDGET CONTINUED

Month:___________

Clothing

Adults: $_______

Kids: $_______

Cleaning/Laundry/Repairs $_______

Other____________: $_______

Transportation

Car payment: $_______

Gas: $_______

Repairs/Maintenance: $_______

Public transportation: $_______

Other____________: $_______

Health & Medicine

Medication: $_______

Doctor Bills: $_______

Copay: $_______

Pets: $_______

Other____________: $_______

Insurances

Health Insurance: $_______

Life Insurance: $_______

Homeowner/Renter: $_______

Auto Insurance: $_______

Other policies____________: $_______

Personal

Personal Care/Grooming: $_______

Toiletries $_______

Tuition Fees: $_______

Books/Supplies: $_______

Child Care/Babysitter: $_______

MONTHLY BUDGET

Monthly Income **Month:___________**

Income (Source 1): $_______

Income (Source 2): $_______

Total Monthly Income: $_______

Charity

Tithe/Giving: $_______

Saving

Emergency Fund: $_______

Retirement Fund: $_______

Housing

Mortgage/Rent: $_______

Real Estate Taxes: $_______

Maintenance/Repairs: $_______

Association Dues: $_______

Utilities

Electric/Gas: $_______

Water: $_______

Phone: $_______

Internet: $_______

Cable: $_______

Other____________: $_______

Food

Groceries: $_______

Takeout: $_______

MONTHLY BUDGET CONTINUED

Month:___________

Clothing

Adults:	$______
Kids:	$______
Cleaning/Laundry/Repairs	$______
Other____________:	$______

Transportation

Car payment:	$______
Gas:	$______
Repairs/Maintenance:	$______
Public transportation:	$______
Other____________:	$______

Health & Medicine

Medication:	$______
Doctor Bills:	$______
Copay:	$______
Pets:	$______
Other____________:	$______

Insurances

Health Insurance:	$______
Life Insurance:	$______
Homeowner/Renter:	$______
Auto Insurance:	$______
Other policies____________:	$______

Personal

Personal Care/Grooming:	$______
Toiletries	$______
Tuition Fees:	$______
Books/Supplies:	$______
Child Care/Babysitter:	$______

MONTHLY BUDGET

Month:___________

Monthly Income

Income (Source 1): $_______

Income (Source 2): $_______

Total Monthly Income: $_______

Charity

Tithe/Giving: $_______

Saving

Emergency Fund: $_______

Retirement Fund: $_______

Housing

Mortgage/Rent: $_______

Real Estate Taxes: $_______

Maintenance/Repairs: $_______

Association Dues: $_______

Utilities

Electric/Gas: $_______

Water: $_______

Phone: $_______

Internet: $_______

Cable: $_______

Other____________: $_______

Food

Groceries: $_______

Takeout: $_______

MONTHLY BUDGET CONTINUED

Month:___________

Clothing

Adults: $_______
Kids: $_______
Cleaning/Laundry/Repairs $_______
Other____________: : $_______

Transportation

Car payment: $_______
Gas: $_______
Repairs/Maintenance: $_______
Public transportation: $_______
Other____________: $_______

Health & Medicine

Medication: $_______
Doctor Bills: $_______
Copay: $_______
Pets: $_______
Other____________: $_______

Insurances

Health Insurance: $_______
Life Insurance: $_______
Homeowner/Renter: $_______
Auto Insurance: $_______
Other policies____________: $_______

Personal

Personal Care/Grooming: $_______
Toiletries $_______
Tuition Fees: $_______
Books/Supplies: $_______
Child Care/Babysitter: $_______

MONTHLY BUDGET

Monthly Income **Month:___________**

Income (Source 1): $_______

Income (Source 2): $_______

Total Monthly Income: $_______

Charity

Tithe/Giving: $_______

Saving

Emergency Fund: $_______

Retirement Fund: $_______

Housing

Mortgage/Rent: $_______

Real Estate Taxes: $_______

Maintenance/Repairs: $_______

Association Dues: $_______

Utilities

Electric/Gas: $_______

Water: $_______

Phone: $_______

Internet: $_______

Cable: $_______

Other___________: $_______

Food

Groceries: $_______

Takeout: $_______

MONTHLY BUDGET CONTINUED

Month:___________

Clothing

Adults:	$_______
Kids:	$_______
Cleaning/Laundry/Repairs	$_______
Other____________: :	$_______

Transportation

Car payment:	$_______
Gas:	$_______
Repairs/Maintenance:	$_______
Public transportation:	$_______
Other____________:	$_______

Health & Medicine

Medication:	$_______
Doctor Bills:	$_______
Copay:	$_______
Pets:	$_______
Other____________:	$_______

Insurances

Health Insurance:	$_______
Life Insurance:	$_______
Homeowner/Renter:	$_______
Auto Insurance:	$_______
Other policies____________:	$_______

Personal

Personal Care/Grooming:	$_______
Toiletries	$_______
Tuition Fees:	$_______
Books/Supplies:	$_______
Child Care/Babysitter:	$_______

MONTHLY BUDGET

Monthly Income **Month:**___________

Income (Source 1): $_______

Income (Source 2): $_______

Total Monthly Income: $_______

Charity

Tithe/Giving: $_______

Saving

Emergency Fund: $_______

Retirement Fund: $_______

Housing

Mortgage/Rent: $_______

Real Estate Taxes: $_______

Maintenance/Repairs: $_______

Association Dues: $_______

Utilities

Electric/Gas: $_______

Water: $_______

Phone: $_______

Internet: $_______

Cable: $_______

Other____________: $_______

Food

Groceries: $_______

Takeout: $_______

MONTHLY BUDGET CONTINUED

Month:___________

Clothing

Adults: $________
Kids: $________
Cleaning/Laundry/Repairs $________
Other____________: : $________

Transportation

Car payment: $________
Gas: $________
Repairs/Maintenance: $________
Public transportation: $________
Other____________: $________

Health & Medicine

Medication: $________
Doctor Bills: $________
Copay: $________
Pets: $________
Other____________: $________

Insurances

Health Insurance: $________
Life Insurance: $________
Homeowner/Renter: $________
Auto Insurance: $________
Other policies____________: $________

Personal

Personal Care/Grooming: $________
Toiletries $________
Tuition Fees: $________
Books/Supplies: $________
Child Care/Babysitter: $________

MONTHLY BUDGET

Monthly Income **Month:___________**

Income (Source 1):	$_______
Income (Source 2):	$_______
Total Monthly Income:	$_______
Charity	
Tithe/Giving:	$_______
Saving	
Emergency Fund:	$_______
Retirement Fund:	$_______
Housing	
Mortgage/Rent:	$_______
Real Estate Taxes:	$_______
Maintenance/Repairs:	$_______
Association Dues:	$_______
Utilities	
Electric/Gas:	$_______
Water:	$_______
Phone:	$_______
Internet:	$_______
Cable:	$_______
Other____________:	$_______
Food	
Groceries:	$_______
Takeout:	$_______

MONTHLY BUDGET CONTINUED

Month:___________

Clothing

Adults: $_______
Kids: $_______
Cleaning/Laundry/Repairs $_______
Other____________: : $_______

Transportation

Car payment: $_______
Gas: $_______
Repairs/Maintenance: $_______
Public transportation: $_______
Other____________: $_______

Health & Medicine

Medication: $_______
Doctor Bills: $_______
Copay: $_______
Pets: $_______
Other____________: $_______

Insurances

Health Insurance: $_______
Life Insurance: $_______
Homeowner/Renter: $_______
Auto Insurance: $_______
Other policies____________: $_______

Personal

Personal Care/Grooming: $_______
Toiletries $_______
Tuition Fees: $_______
Books/Supplies: $_______
Child Care/Babysitter: $_______

MONTHLY BUDGET

Month:___________

Monthly Income

Income (Source 1): $_______

Income (Source 2): $_______

Total Monthly Income: $_______

Charity

Tithe/Giving: $_______

Saving

Emergency Fund: $_______

Retirement Fund: $_______

Housing

Mortgage/Rent: $_______

Real Estate Taxes: $_______

Maintenance/Repairs: $_______

Association Dues: $_______

Utilities

Electric/Gas: $_______

Water: $_______

Phone: $_______

Internet: $_______

Cable: $_______

Other____________: $_______

Food

Groceries: $_______

Takeout: $_______

MONTHLY BUDGET CONTINUED

Month:___________

Clothing

Adults: $_______
Kids: $_______
Cleaning/Laundry/Repairs $_______
Other____________: $_______

Transportation

Car payment: $_______
Gas: $_______
Repairs/Maintenance: $_______
Public transportation: $_______
Other____________: $_______

Health & Medicine

Medication: $_______
Doctor Bills: $_______
Copay: $_______
Pets: $_______
Other____________: $_______

Insurances

Health Insurance: $_______
Life Insurance: $_______
Homeowner/Renter: $_______
Auto Insurance: $_______
Other policies_____________: $_______

Personal

Personal Care/Grooming: $_______
Toiletries $_______
Tuition Fees: $_______
Books/Supplies: $_______
Child Care/Babysitter: $_______

MONTHLY BUDGET

Monthly Income **Month:___________**

Income (Source 1): $_______

Income (Source 2): $_______

Total Monthly Income: $_______

Charity

Tithe/Giving: $_______

Saving

Emergency Fund: $_______

Retirement Fund: $_______

Housing

Mortgage/Rent: $_______

Real Estate Taxes: $_______

Maintenance/Repairs: $_______

Association Dues: $_______

Utilities

Electric/Gas: $_______

Water: $_______

Phone: $_______

Internet: $_______

Cable: $_______

Other___________: $_______

Food

Groceries: $_______

Takeout: $_______

MONTHLY BUDGET CONTINUED

Month:___________

Clothing

Adults: $_______
Kids: $_______
Cleaning/Laundry/Repairs $_______
Other_____________: $_______

Transportation

Car payment: $_______
Gas: $_______
Repairs/Maintenance: $_______
Public transportation: $_______
Other_____________: $_______

Health & Medicine

Medication: $_______
Doctor Bills: $_______
Copay: $_______
Pets: $_______
Other_____________: $_______

Insurances

Health Insurance: $_______
Life Insurance: $_______
Homeowner/Renter: $_______
Auto Insurance: $_______
Other policies______________: $_______

Personal

Personal Care/Grooming: $_______
Toiletries $_______
Tuition Fees: $_______
Books/Supplies: $_______
Child Care/Babysitter: $_______

MONTHLY BUDGET

Monthly Income **Month:____________**

Income (Source 1): $________

Income (Source 2): $________

Total Monthly Income: $________

Charity

Tithe/Giving: $________

Saving

Emergency Fund: $________

Retirement Fund: $________

Housing

Mortgage/Rent: $________

Real Estate Taxes: $________

Maintenance/Repairs: $________

Association Dues: $________

Utilities

Electric/Gas: $________

Water: $________

Phone: $________

Internet: $________

Cable: $________

Other____________: $________

Food

Groceries: $________

Takeout: $________

MONTHLY BUDGET CONTINUED

Month:___________

Clothing

Adults: $_______

Kids: $_______

Cleaning/Laundry/Repairs $_______

Other____________: : $_______

Transportation

Car payment: $_______

Gas: $_______

Repairs/Maintenance: $_______

Public transportation: $_______

Other____________: $_______

Health & Medicine

Medication: $_______

Doctor Bills: $_______

Copay: $_______

Pets: $_______

Other____________: $_______

Insurances

Health Insurance: $_______

Life Insurance: $_______

Homeowner/Renter: $_______

Auto Insurance: $_______

Other policies____________: $_______

Personal

Personal Care/Grooming: $_______

Toiletries $_______

Tuition Fees: $_______

Books/Supplies: $_______

Child Care/Babysitter: $_______

MONTHLY BUDGET

Month:____________

Monthly Income

Income (Source 1): $_______

Income (Source 2): $_______

Total Monthly Income: $_______

Charity

Tithe/Giving: $_______

Saving

Emergency Fund: $_______

Retirement Fund: $_______

Housing

Mortgage/Rent: $_______

Real Estate Taxes: $_______

Maintenance/Repairs: $_______

Association Dues: $_______

Utilities

Electric/Gas: $_______

Water: $_______

Phone: $_______

Internet: $_______

Cable: $_______

Other____________: $_______

Food

Groceries: $_______

Takeout: $_______

MONTHLY BUDGET CONTINUED

Month:___________

Clothing

Adults: $______

Kids: $______

Cleaning/Laundry/Repairs $______

Other____________: $______

Transportation

Car payment: $______

Gas: $______

Repairs/Maintenance: $______

Public transportation: $______

Other____________: $______

Health & Medicine

Medication: $______

Doctor Bills: $______

Copay: $______

Pets: $______

Other____________: $______

Insurances

Health Insurance: $______

Life Insurance: $______

Homeowner/Renter: $______

Auto Insurance: $______

Other policies____________: $______

Personal

Personal Care/Grooming: $______

Toiletries $______

Tuition Fees: $______

Books/Supplies: $______

Child Care/Babysitter: $______

MONTHLY BUDGET

Month:___________

Monthly Income

Income (Source 1): $_______

Income (Source 2): $_______

Total Monthly Income: $_______

Charity

Tithe/Giving: $_______

Saving

Emergency Fund: $_______

Retirement Fund: $_______

Housing

Mortgage/Rent: $_______

Real Estate Taxes: $_______

Maintenance/Repairs: $_______

Association Dues: $_______

Utilities

Electric/Gas: $_______

Water: $_______

Phone: $_______

Internet: $_______

Cable: $_______

Other___________: $_______

Food

Groceries: $_______

Takeout: $_______

MONTHLY BUDGET CONTINUED

Month:___________

Clothing

Adults:	$_______
Kids:	$_______
Cleaning/Laundry/Repairs	$_______
Other____________: :	$_______

Transportation

Car payment:	$_______
Gas:	$_______
Repairs/Maintenance:	$_______
Public transportation:	$_______
Other____________:	$_______

Health & Medicine

Medication:	$_______
Doctor Bills:	$_______
Copay:	$_______
Pets:	$_______
Other____________:	$_______

Insurances

Health Insurance:	$_______
Life Insurance:	$_______
Homeowner/Renter:	$_______
Auto Insurance:	$_______
Other policies_____________:	$_______

Personal

Personal Care/Grooming:	$_______
Toiletries	$_______
Tuition Fees:	$_______
Books/Supplies:	$_______
Child Care/Babysitter:	$_______

MONTHLY BUDGET

Month:___________

Monthly Income

Income (Source 1): $_______

Income (Source 2): $_______

Total Monthly Income: $_______

Charity

Tithe/Giving: $_______

Saving

Emergency Fund: $_______

Retirement Fund: $_______

Housing $_______

Mortgage/Rent:

Real Estate Taxes: $_______

Maintenance/Repairs: $_______

Association Dues: $_______

Utilities

Electric/Gas: $_______

Water: $_______

Phone: $_______

Internet: $_______

Cable: $_______

Other___________: $_______

Food

Groceries: $_______

Takeout: $_______

MONTHLY BUDGET CONTINUED

Month:___________

Clothing	
Adults:	$_______
Kids:	$_______
Cleaning/Laundry/Repairs	$_______
Other____________: :	$_______
Transportation	
Car payment:	$_______
Gas:	$_______
Repairs/Maintenance:	$_______
Public transportation:	$_______
Other____________:	$_______
Health & Medicine	
Medication:	$_______
Doctor Bills:	$_______
Copay:	$_______
Pets:	$_______
Other____________:	$_______
Insurances	
Health Insurance:	$_______
Life Insurance:	$_______
Homeowner/Renter:	$_______
Auto Insurance:	$_______
Other policies_____________:	$_______
Personal	
Personal Care/Grooming:	$_______
Toiletries	$_______
Tuition Fees:	$_______
Books/Supplies:	$_______
Child Care/Babysitter:	$_______

MONTHLY BUDGET

Monthly Income **Month:__________**

Income (Source 1): $_______

Income (Source 2): $_______

Total Monthly Income: $_______

Charity

Tithe/Giving: $_______

Saving

Emergency Fund: $_______

Retirement Fund: $_______

Housing

Mortgage/Rent: $_______

Real Estate Taxes: $_______

Maintenance/Repairs: $_______

Association Dues: $_______

Utilities

Electric/Gas: $_______

Water: $_______

Phone: $_______

Internet: $_______

Cable: $_______

Other___________: $_______

Food

Groceries: $_______

Takeout: $_______

MONTHLY BUDGET CONTINUED

Month:___________

Clothing

Adults: $_______

Kids: $_______

Cleaning/Laundry/Repairs $_______

Other____________: : $_______

Transportation

Car payment: $_______

Gas: $_______

Repairs/Maintenance: $_______

Public transportation: $_______

Other____________: $_______

Health & Medicine

Medication: $_______

Doctor Bills: $_______

Copay: $_______

Pets: $_______

Other____________: $_______

Insurances

Health Insurance: $_______

Life Insurance: $_______

Homeowner/Renter: $_______

Auto Insurance: $_______

Other policies____________: $_______

Personal

Personal Care/Grooming: $_______

Toiletries $_______

Tuition Fees: $_______

Books/Supplies: $_______

Child Care/Babysitter: $_______

MONTHLY BUDGET

Month:__________

Monthly Income

Income (Source 1): $________

Income (Source 2): $________

Total Monthly Income: $________

Charity

Tithe/Giving: $________

Saving

Emergency Fund: $________

Retirement Fund: $________

Housing

Mortgage/Rent: $________

Real Estate Taxes: $________

Maintenance/Repairs: $________

Association Dues: $________

Utilities

Electric/Gas: $________

Water: $________

Phone: $________

Internet: $________

Cable: $________

Other____________: $________

Food

Groceries: $________

Takeout: $________

MONTHLY BUDGET CONTINUED

Month:___________

Clothing

Adults: $_______
Kids: $_______
Cleaning/Laundry/Repairs $_______
Other____________: : $_______

Transportation

Car payment: $_______
Gas: $_______
Repairs/Maintenance: $_______
Public transportation: $_______
Other____________: $_______

Health & Medicine

Medication: $_______
Doctor Bills: $_______
Copay: $_______
Pets: $_______
Other____________: $_______

Insurances

Health Insurance: $_______
Life Insurance: $_______
Homeowner/Renter: $_______
Auto Insurance: $_______
Other policies_____________: $_______

Personal

Personal Care/Grooming: $_______
Toiletries $_______
Tuition Fees: $_______
Books/Supplies: $_______
Child Care/Babysitter: $_______

MONTHLY BUDGET

Month:___________

Monthly Income

Income (Source 1): $_______

Income (Source 2): $_______

Total Monthly Income: $_______

Charity

Tithe/Giving: $_______

Saving

Emergency Fund: $_______

Retirement Fund: $_______

Housing

Mortgage/Rent: $_______

Real Estate Taxes: $_______

Maintenance/Repairs: $_______

Association Dues: $_______

Utilities

Electric/Gas: $_______

Water: $_______

Phone: $_______

Internet: $_______

Cable: $_______

Other____________: $_______

Food

Groceries: $_______

Takeout: $_______

MONTHLY BUDGET CONTINUED

Month:____________

Clothing

Adults: $_______

Kids: $_______

Cleaning/Laundry/Repairs $_______

Other____________: $_______

Transportation

Car payment: $_______

Gas: $_______

Repairs/Maintenance: $_______

Public transportation: $_______

Other____________: $_______

Health & Medicine

Medication: $_______

Doctor Bills: $_______

Copay: $_______

Pets: $_______

Other____________: $_______

Insurances

Health Insurance: $_______

Life Insurance: $_______

Homeowner/Renter: $_______

Auto Insurance: $_______

Other policies____________: $_______

Personal

Personal Care/Grooming: $_______

Toiletries $_______

Tuition Fees: $_______

Books/Supplies: $_______

Child Care/Babysitter: $_______

MONTHLY BUDGET

Monthly Income **Month:___________**

Income (Source 1): $_______
Income (Source 2): $_______
Total Monthly Income: $_______

Charity
Tithe/Giving: $_______

Saving
Emergency Fund: $_______
Retirement Fund: $_______

Housing
Mortgage/Rent: $_______
Real Estate Taxes: $_______
Maintenance/Repairs: $_______
Association Dues: $_______

Utilities
Electric/Gas: $_______
Water: $_______
Phone: $_______
Internet: $_______
Cable: $_______
Other___________: $_______

Food
Groceries: $_______
Takeout: $_______

MONTHLY BUDGET CONTINUED

Month:___________

Clothing

Adults:	$______
Kids:	$______
Cleaning/Laundry/Repairs	$______
Other____________:	$______

Transportation

Car payment:	$______
Gas:	$______
Repairs/Maintenance:	$______
Public transportation:	$______
Other____________:	$______

Health & Medicine

Medication:	$______
Doctor Bills:	$______
Copay:	$______
Pets:	$______
Other____________:	$______

Insurances

Health Insurance:	$______
Life Insurance:	$______
Homeowner/Renter:	$______
Auto Insurance:	$______
Other policies____________:	$______

Personal

Personal Care/Grooming:	$______
Toiletries	$______
Tuition Fees:	$______
Books/Supplies:	$______
Child Care/Babysitter:	$______

MONTHLY BUDGET

Monthly Income Month:___________

Income (Source 1): $________

Income (Source 2): $________

Total Monthly Income: $________

Charity

Tithe/Giving: $________

Saving

Emergency Fund: $________

Retirement Fund: $________

Housing

Mortgage/Rent: $________

Real Estate Taxes: $________

Maintenance/Repairs: $________

Association Dues: $________

Utilities

Electric/Gas: $________

Water: $________

Phone: $________

Internet: $________

Cable: $________

Other____________: $________

Food

Groceries: $________

Takeout: $________

MONTHLY BUDGET CONTINUED

Month:___________

Clothing

Adults: $_______

Kids: $_______

Cleaning/Laundry/Repairs $_______

Other____________: : $_______

Transportation

Car payment: $_______

Gas: $_______

Repairs/Maintenance: $_______

Public transportation: $_______

Other____________: $_______

Health & Medicine

Medication: $_______

Doctor Bills: $_______

Copay: $_______

Pets: $_______

Other____________: $_______

Insurances

Health Insurance: $_______

Life Insurance: $_______

Homeowner/Renter: $_______

Auto Insurance: $_______

Other policies_____________: $_______

Personal

Personal Care/Grooming: $_______

Toiletries $_______

Tuition Fees: $_______

Books/Supplies: $_______

Child Care/Babysitter: $_______

MONTHLY BUDGET

Monthly Income **Month:__________**

Income (Source 1): $_______
Income (Source 2): $_______
Total Monthly Income: $_______

Charity
Tithe/Giving: $_______

Saving
Emergency Fund: $_______
Retirement Fund: $_______

Housing
Mortgage/Rent: $_______
Real Estate Taxes: $_______
Maintenance/Repairs: $_______
Association Dues: $_______

Utilities
Electric/Gas: $_______
Water: $_______
Phone: $_______
Internet: $_______
Cable: $_______
Other____________: $_______

Food
Groceries: $_______
Takeout: $_______

MONTHLY BUDGET CONTINUED

Month:___________

Clothing

Adults:	$_______
Kids:	$_______
Cleaning/Laundry/Repairs	$_______
Other____________: :	$_______

Transportation

Car payment:	$_______
Gas:	$_______
Repairs/Maintenance:	$_______
Public transportation:	$_______
Other____________:	$_______

Health & Medicine

Medication:	$_______
Doctor Bills:	$_______
Copay:	$_______
Pets:	$_______
Other____________:	$_______

Insurances

Health Insurance:	$_______
Life Insurance:	$_______
Homeowner/Renter:	$_______
Auto Insurance:	$_______
Other policies____________:	$_______

Personal

Personal Care/Grooming:	$_______
Toiletries	$_______
Tuition Fees:	$_______
Books/Supplies:	$_______
Child Care/Babysitter:	$_______

Made in the USA
Monee, IL
04 November 2026

67375603R00069